The "Fa:
General Editors: (

G000296002

SOMEONE TO
TALK TO

THE STORY OF CHAD VARAH
AND THE SAMARITANS

Audrey Constant

THE RELIGIOUS EDUCATION PRESS
A Division of Pergamon Press

The Religious Education Press
A Division of Pergamon Press
Hennock Road, Exeter EX2 8RP

Pergamon Press Ltd
Headington Hill Hall, Oxford OX3 0BW

Pergamon Press Inc.
Maxwell House, Fairview Park, Elmsford, New York 10523

Pergamon Press Canada Ltd
Suite 104, 150 Consumers Road, Willowdale, Ontario M2J 1P9

Pergamon Press (Australia) Pty Ltd
P.O. Box 544, Potts Point, N.S.W. 2011

Pergamon Press GmbH
Hammerweg 6, D-6242 Kronberg, Federal Republic of Germany

Photographs are reproduced by courtesy of Maria Bartha
(pp. 11, 13, 17), K. Biggar (pp. 12, 19), Hart Associates Ltd
(p. 7) and The Revd Chad Varah (p. 20).

First published 1981

Printed in Great Britain by A. Wheaton & Co. Ltd, Exeter

ISBN 0 08-026417-4 non net
ISBN 0 08-026418-2 net

SOMEONE TO TALK TO

The Story of Chad Varah
and the Samaritans

One day in 1936 a priest called Chad Varah was taking the funeral of a thirteen-year-old girl. It was pouring with rain and there were only a few people there: the men who carried the coffin, the young priest and one or two others.

As Chad walked beside the coffin he learned why this young girl had died. She had not been ill. Fear had driven her to despair. When she had her first monthly period, she thought she had some dreadful disease. She did not know what was happening to her. Because there was no one she felt she could talk to, she did not tell anyone about her secret. In the end she could bear it no longer, so she killed herself.

Since the girl had no one to talk to, there was no way she could find out what was happening to her. It was just a normal part of growing up, but to the girl it had become a terrifying experience.

The young priest was shocked at the waste of such a young life. If only the girl had been able to talk to someone – even a stranger – her life could have been saved.

As Chad buried her, he made a promise. "Little girl," he said, "I never knew you, but you have changed my life." He decided to take every chance he could to talk to young people about their problems.

His early life

Chad Varah was brought up in a Christian home, the eldest of a large family. His father was a clergyman and he wanted Chad to become one, too. But while Chad was growing up, although he often went to church, he was not sure what he believed.

He liked science at school, and was good at it. He carried on his studies at university. But when he graduated from university, he still had no idea what he wanted to do with his life.

For a while Chad helped in a home for handicapped children. He did the washing-up and played with the children. Later on he worked for a firm that made bricks, doing chemical research. At the same time he earned extra money by writing articles for newspapers.

At about this time, Chad went to see an uncle of his who had been a missionary in Africa. Chad enjoyed talking to him, even though his uncle was much older than himself. Chad called him his *guru*, which is the Indian word for "teacher". He discussed his future with his uncle.

"Why don't you become a priest?" asked his uncle. "After all, you don't have a better idea, do you?"

By now God meant very much more to Chad. He went to a college in Lincoln and trained for the priesthood. He was taught by Michael Ramsay, who later became Archbishop of Canterbury. It was he who helped Chad to see that God wanted him to be a priest.

2

The youth club

Two years later, Chad finished his training and went to St Giles's Church in Lincoln. There, among other things, he ran a youth club. He spent hours talking to the youngsters at the coffee bar and playing table tennis with them. To begin with they boasted about all the trouble they got into and tried out their bad language on him.

Far from shocking him, they found Chad wanted to listen and was interested in what they had to say. Their swearing did not seem to upset him at all. They agreed that, on the whole, Chad was quite a likeable fellow. Soon they came to him, one by one, and told him about their problems. They were surprised at how understanding he was.

Chad also gave sex education classes to engaged couples. He worked with a very wise priest who helped him, even though some of his parishioners did not like what he was doing. They told him, "Vicar, you ought to stop that young priest giving those talks to our young people."

The vicar replied, "My guess is that one day similar talks will be given in every church in the country." He knew how important Chad's classes were to those couples, and how natural and beautiful Chad made sex sound.

By now, not only young people from his own church came to hear him, but also others from nearby churches.

Children's comics

From St Giles's Chad was sent to other churches. He was always more interested in working among young people than in doing any other kind of church work.

Towards the end of the Second World War, he went to St Paul's Church, Clapham Junction, in South London.

3

He was also the visiting priest at St John's Hospital, Battersea. While he was there he met a clergyman friend of his called Marcus Morris. Morris was starting a children's comic called *Eagle*. It had plenty of picture stories and articles about famous people, as well as puzzles. Before long, *Eagle* was being read by children all over the country.

Morris asked Chad to help him with this comic. As he was good at science, one of Chad's jobs was to see that Dan Dare, the space hero, did not do anything that was scientifically impossible. For instance, he could not travel faster than the speed of light.

Another job Chad was given was to write the back page story about the life of St Paul. Going home on the bus one day, he read the story of Paul in the Bible. A strange thing happened. Every scene in the story sprang to life as though he were there himself. When he arrived home he got out a piece of paper; on one side he wrote the words of the story, and on the other, ideas for pictures for the artist to follow.

There are very few people who can see scenes so clearly in their minds. They are called "visualisers". Morris was very pleased to find that Chad had this gift, and he kept him busy thinking up pictures for stories. *Eagle* was so successful that it was soon followed by other comics, like *Girl*, *Swift* and *Robin*.

For twelve years Chad went on working for the Church and writing for children's comics. At the same time he wrote articles for newspapers about other things that concerned him deeply.

Chad knew that many people live with secret fears, or struggle to cope with some kind of behaviour of which they are ashamed. They are often too embarrassed to discuss their problem, or to seek expert help. Chad wrote about such problems in a very helpful and sympathetic way.

4

Many of these articles were read by people with similar troubles. It set their minds at rest to know that they were not alone, and that other people suffered in the same way as they did. Chad did not criticise them, but was understanding and helpful. They wrote to or telephoned him, asking for advice with their own problems.

Some people, he discovered, were so worried that they did not want to go on living. In what little time he had, he tried to help them by talking to them over the telephone or replying to their letters. Some needed more time, and these he invited to come and see him.

Chad was happiest when meeting people one at a time: in a sick-room, a hospital, or a prison cell. He found he was able to help them. He wanted to give all his time to this sort of work.

Chad felt that God was guiding him in this direction. He had an idea that God has a special way of making us do things: He does not shout instructions through a heavenly loudspeaker; instead, He makes all of us especially good at something, then guides us to use these gifts. In other words, God's call is a challenge to us to find out what we are *for*.

Chad felt at last he knew what *he* was here for. He read that there were three suicides every day in Greater London. To him these were not simply numbers. They were people he could imagine dying miserably in lonely rooms, with some secret fear or a broken heart. Life had become so hard for them that they could no longer bear it. He was determined to try to help them, if they wanted to be helped. If not, he knew he had no right to interfere.

But how was he to get in touch with these people? And how would they find him? The quickest way would be by telephone. Even those who did not have their own phone could use a telephone-box. This way they could remain unseen and unknown if they wanted to.

5

But how could Chad do this and run his church at the same time? It seemed an impossible task. He had a talk with God. "There must be someone else," he argued. "I'm busy. I have a church to run and my hospital work to do. I have my writing, and a wife and four children to keep."

What he really needed was a church without too many parishioners to care for. Then he would have more time.

A small miracle

There are some London churches that are well-endowed. This means that at some time in the past rich people left them enough money to pay for the running of the church and to pay the clergymen who served there. The Church of St Stephen, Walbrook, in the City of London, is one such church. In 1953 Chad was invited to be the Rector of St Stephen's.

St Stephen's is the parish church of the Lord Mayor of London. It is next door to the Mansion House, the official home of the Lord Mayor. The church was built by the great architect, Sir Christopher Wren. Badly bombed during the war, it was later restored.

Luckily for Chad, St Stephen's had only a few parishioners. This was because few people actually live in the City of London, although over a million people work there during the day.

Chad accepted the job. He decided to set up his telephone service in a small room in the church.

In October 1953 he rang the Telephone Exchange Supervisor to discuss choosing a suitable telephone number for the service. In those days, not many people had telephones, and you could sometimes choose your own telephone number.

6

Chad Varah with a client at St. Stephen's Church, 1965

Chad wanted a number that was easy to remember, like the 999 emergency number of the police, fire and ambulance services.

"How about something simple, with a nine in it?" he asked the supervisor.

The supervisor said she thought all those sorts of numbers were in use already, but said she could check for him.

"I would like Mansion House 9000," he said, "but I suppose someone has that number."

"I expect so," she agreed. "What is your number at the moment?"

Chad dusted off the dial of the telephone in the shabby little room.

"It's all right!" he cried. "It's Mansion House 9000!"

So, with this small miracle, in the midst of the rubble left by the war, he began his work of caring for people with fears and problems.

Why "The Samaritans"?

At last Chad had a base to operate from and an income to live on while he worked. And he had a telephone. Now he needed a name for his project.

He thought of the story of the Good Samaritan in the Bible, about a man who lay wounded and dying on a dusty road in Palestine. Everyone passed him by. They did not want to have anything to do with him. They did not want to get involved.

Then the Samaritan arrived. Although he was a stranger in those parts, he did not hesitate. He went across to the man, gave him water and bound up his wounds. Then he put him on his donkey and took him to the nearest inn, where they looked after him.

Like the Samaritan, Chad wanted to help people who had no one else to turn to. Inspired by the story, he decided to call his organisation "The Samaritans".

All that was needed now was for the newspapers to make the telephone number and service widely known. Then he would try to cope with the result. Again Chad found people ready to help. Newspapers all over the country printed the story of his work. Soon the telephone began to ring.

In need of a friend

The calls came from people of all ages and with every kind of problem. Most of them were ordinary people who had come to a crisis in their lives. Some of them had been driven to despair; others were almost ready to commit suicide. Many of them were having difficulties with their marriages. Others had lost someone they loved or depended on. There were people with drink problems. A few were mentally ill and needed expert help.

Chad listened to them all. After speaking to them over the telephone he found that many of them wanted to come and see him personally. He could not always give them enough help with just one telephone call.

Chad worked the whole day through. Sometimes he had eleven one-hour interviews in a day. Often he had to stop an interview to answer a telephone call. He did not even have time for meals. Although he had a secretary to deal with the business side of things, he was the only one who could advise these people. As a clergyman he was used to giving advice.

Just when he was wondering how he was going to manage if things went on like this, he received offers of help. These volunteers were ordinary people who did not have any special training, but who had heard of Chad's work and how busy he was. They wanted to use what time they had to help him. Some were housewives who had some spare time during the day when their children were at school. Others only had spare time in the evenings after work.

Chad did not immediately see how he could use these kind people, but he did not want to turn them away. Perhaps they could look after his visitors (or clients, as he called them) while they waited to see him.

It was the volunteers, not Chad, who discovered how they could help. They turned up regularly; they made coffee and talked kindly to the clients, making them feel relaxed and comfortable. And often, as they had more time than Chad did, they made a better job of comforting the clients than he could have done. Some of the clients went away feeling happier, without even seeing Chad. The volunteers had given them the help and comfort they needed.

It didn't take Chad long to realise that what his clients needed was a friend, not expert advice. They wanted someone to listen to their troubles and care about them until their difficult time was over.

Chad knew that volunteers would have to be carefully chosen and prepared for the work, but his helpers had already shown they had the qualities needed to make good Samaritans. They had offered friendship at a time of loneliness and fear.

Soon the little room where Chad had begun his telephone service became too small for him and his helpers. It was then that he discovered an old burial vault right under the church. A group of people who were interested in Chad's work paid the cost of turning the vault into rooms from which The Samaritans could operate. It was also agreed that The Samaritans could always have the use of these rooms, whoever the Rector of St Stephen's might be in years to come.

As time went by, more and more Samaritan centres were opened. In 1980 there were 170 branches of The Samaritans and 20 000 volunteers in the United Kingdom and the Republic of Ireland. Every year over 250 000 people contact The Samaritans for the first time, and well over a million people call or visit Samaritan centres.

What sort of people become volunteers?

People from all walks of life volunteer to become Samaritans. They range from factory workers to company directors, and from teenagers to grandparents. Anyone over the age of seventeen can apply.

The volunteers are not necessarily Christians, because The Samaritans are a non-religious organisation. They all have one thing in common, though: they want to help people in distress.

Volunteers have to be chosen carefully, because it is not easy to help people in despair. They must be patient, ready to listen to people's troubles. They have to be able to keep to the rules they accept when they become Samaritans. They have to be reliable and not be put off by rudeness. (When people are upset they can sometimes be rude.) Chad says, "We want those who really care, who can listen and who are humble enough to do anything for us."

About forty per cent of all applicants become Samaritans. After they have been selected, they have to go through a preparation course, followed by a trial period of several months. Only then can they be accepted as Samaritan volunteers.

Arnold, The Samaritans' coach

A Samaritan centre at work

A Samaritan centre usually has three telephones. Two are for clients and the other one is for ordinary business, like running the branch. The centre is manned twenty-four hours a day, every day of the year. There may be three or four volunteers on duty (more in a busy branch). They work in shifts of three or four hours at a time.

12

A branch is run by a director and deputies, and most branches also have a secretary, a treasurer and a training officer. When expert help is required The Samaritans use consultants. These are lawyers, doctors and specialists upon whom they can call for advice, but only when the client agrees to it.

If there is an emergency and someone has to go to see a client immediately, they use a Flying Squad. Their job is to go, usually at night, to call-boxes, street corners, or wherever quick help is needed.

Sometimes The Samaritans receive a call from someone phoning on behalf of a friend or relative. "My neighbour is very depressed. Please come and help him," they may say. There is a rule about this. The Samaritans believe that everyone should be in charge of their own lives. Unless the call concerns a very young or very old person, or someone who is unable to help themselves, they will not go to them. Instead, they ask the caller to try to persuade that person to telephone The Samaritans themselves, and then they will try to help them.

A client talking to a Samaritan volunteer

Volunteers never ever talk about their clients outside the centre. Whatever passes between the volunteer and his client is private. Clients need not fear that their secrets will be made known.

What sort of people call The Samaritans?

Calls come from ordinary people of all ages who have come to a crisis in their lives. These people are often lonely, because their problem separates them from the rest of the world.

Not everyone has friends and relatives they can talk to when they are troubled. Perhaps the callers' problems are too personal to tell other people about anyway. They might even want to talk *about* their friends or family.

The Samaritans do not only help adults. Many of their clients are under twenty-five, and some of them are school-children. Nor is the organisation only for people who are really desperate or want to commit suicide. Nevertheless, more and more desperate young people are visiting or calling The Samaritans.

The following "case histories" may help to show why people contact The Samaritans. They are not true stories, but show the kinds of problem that arise and how they are dealt with.

Jane had been going out with Don every since she left school. Everyone knew that he was her boy-friend. Although it had never actually been mentioned, Jane felt that it was only a matter of time before they married.

Then one day Jane's cousin, Carol, came to work in the same town. Carol stayed with Jane's family while she looked for somewhere else to live. At first Jane was glad to have Carol. She was fun to be with and she was pretty. Don thought so, too. Although she didn't want to believe it, Jane noticed that Don was soon paying Carol more attention than herself.

Jane hoped that when Carol found a place to live, Don would see less of her and forget her, but it didn't happen that way. It was Jane who saw less of Don and she knew that Carol was taking her place with him.

Jane felt let down and miserable. She did not want to go out with her friends. They all knew about her and Don and she couldn't face them. She could not expect any sympathy from Mum and Dad either. They had never liked Don much. She was desperate.

Then she saw a notice about The Samaritans. She picked up the phone and soon she was telling someone called Eileen all about it. Eileen invited her to the centre. Over a cup of tea, Jane began to feel better. Here was someone who really understood how she felt. Although it did not bring Don back, life somehow did not look quite so bleak any more.

Martin lived with his mother and stepfather, but it was not a happy home. His stepfather never liked him and often lost his temper. Martin did not spend longer than he had to at home. Whenever he could he went out with his friends.

There had been times when they had been in trouble, and although Martin was ready to take a few risks, he didn't like the sort of things they had been up to lately. He didn't want to be accused of chickening out, though. He would lose what friends he had and life would be even lonelier.

One day the gang broke into a shop. Martin hadn't actually gone in, but the police rightly guessed he was one of them. He was let off with a warning.

15

That really frightened him. Where was all this going to lead? He didn't want this sort of life. But if he stayed at home his stepfather would go on at him, and he couldn't stand that. Life was simply not worth living.

He didn't know anything about The Samaritans, but he had seen one of their notices somewhere. Probably they could do nothing for him, he thought, but he was desperate enough to try them. It was quite late at night when he rang. The man's voice at the other end of the line was reassuring. In fact the centre was not far away, so Martin went round for a chat.

After that he called in quite often and talked to Frank. Gradually, with Frank's help, he gained confidence and began to think about what he really wanted to do with his life.

There are particular difficulties about being young – finding friends, discovering about sex, coping at school or with parents at home, becoming independent. Problems always seem worse when you try to bottle them up.

In the end, some people attempt suicide. Few really want to die. They just do not want to live with things as they are.

What happens when a client rings?

When the phone rings in a Samaritan centre, the volunteer on duty answers with the words "The Samaritans – can I help you?" Those six words are very important.

From the sound of the voice, the caller decides whether he can talk to that person about his problem. If he can't, he may put the phone down and try to struggle on alone, or he may wait a while and then ring again. This time perhaps a different voice answers. The client begins to talk.

It may take a long time. The client does not know where

A volunteer on duty at a Samaritan centre

to begin. He may talk about all sorts of other things before he feels he can trust the volunteer enough to tell him the real cause of his despair.

He can talk for as long as he likes. He does not have to give his name if he does not want to. The volunteer tries to put the client at ease, making sure he realises that no one else will know about his problem.

Sometimes just talking things over is enough. At other times decisions have to be made. The volunteer may need to call on other people to help, with the client's permission. Often there is no easy answer to the problem. But the volunteer will not tell the client what to do. He will try to help him to calm down and make up his own mind.

Sometimes the best way a volunteer can help a client is to befriend him. "Befriending" is the Samaritan term for supporting and helping a client. This may mean taking him to visit a doctor, going to the cinema with him, or simply chatting to him over a cup of tea or a pint. Befriending continues until the crisis is over and the client feels ready to cope on his own.

Volunteers often never find out what happens to clients they have spent hours talking with. Sometimes they have no idea whether they were able to help at all. It is enough that they were there to offer warmth and friendship at a time of need.

The Festival Branch

A crowd can be a very lonely place. At pop festivals, for example, where everyone else seems to be having fun, an unhappy person can feel very much alone.

A group of young Samaritans believed they might be able to help in this situation. They formed a team to visit pop festivals. They wanted to find out more about young people's problems by being amongst them.

The Festival Branch has volunteers all over the country. They can be called in at short notice to set up a centre at pop festivals. Most of them are already serving in town branches of The Samaritans or in organisations like Nightlines (student-help services run by students). Often they have to work in noisy, crowded, tense conditions, so most (but not all) of these hundred or so special volunteers are young people.

The Festival Branch operates from a tent which is manned twenty-four hours a day. There are about twenty-five or thirty volunteers in the team, and four to eight

The Samaritans' Festival Tent at Reading Festival

people are usually on duty in any six-hour shift. More are called in if it gets busy – there have been twenty or more volunteers on duty at once in festival tents. When they are off duty the volunteers mingle with the crowds and enjoy the festival like everyone else.

The spread of the Samaritan idea

In 1954 a man who had read about Chad Varah in a newspaper hitch-hiked all the way from Salonika, Greece, to see him. Another time, Chad had a telephone call from a man in Copenhagen, Denmark. The man said he could only afford a three-minute call, and how could he prevent a girl in his office from committing suicide?

Chad said, "I don't need three minutes, just three words: 'Stay with her'."

19

Chad Varah visiting Samaritan volunteers in Bangkok

After an article describing the work of the Samaritans was published in a Swiss magazine, anti-suicide work started in Zurich, and later in West Berlin. Organisers from other countries read similar magazine articles and wrote to Chad asking for advice. And so the idea spread. In 1980 there were about fifty overseas branches in thirty different countries.

These days much of Chad's time is taken up with travelling all over the world, visiting Samaritan centres and giving advice on how they should be run.

Between 1963 and 1977 the suicide rate in England and Wales dropped by about a third. This may have been partly due to The Samaritans. Now, sadly, suicide and attempted suicide are on the increase again. The Samaritans get busier and busier.

BIOGRAPHICAL NOTES

Chad Varah was born on 12 November 1911, the eldest son of the Vicar of Barton-on-Humber, Humberside.

He was educated at Worksop College, Nottinghamshire, and later obtained a scholarship to Keble College, Oxford, where he studied Natural Sciences. After his graduation in 1933 he trained for the priesthood at Lincoln Theological College.

Between 1935 and 1942 Chad Varah worked as a curate in churches in Lincoln, London and Barrow-in-Furness. He was appointed Vicar of Holy Trinity Church, Blackburn, in 1942. In 1949 he became Vicar of St Paul's Church, Clapham Junction, in London. Since 1953 he has been Rector of the Church of St Stephen, Walbrook, in the City of London, the parish church of the Lord Mayor of London.

From 1950 to 1961 Chad Varah worked as Scriptwriter and Visualiser for *Eagle* and *Girl* comics as well as carrying out his Church duties.

In 1953 he founded The Samaritans, an organisation to help the despairing and suicidal. The first branch of The Samaritans was set up at St Stephen's, in the City of London. In 1980 there were 170 branches of The Samaritans in the United Kingdom and the Republic of Ireland, dealing with over a million calls and visits a year.

Chad Varah was the Director of the London branch of The Samaritans until 1974, when he became its President.

Chad Varah's awards and prizes include the O.B.E. (Officer of the Order of the British Empire), the Albert Schweitzer Gold Medal, the Prix de l'Institut de la Vie and the Roumanian Patriarchal Cross.

THINGS TO DO

A Test yourself

Here are some short questions. See if you can remember the answers from what you have read. Then write them down in a few words.

1 When he was at school, which subject was Chad good at?
2 Which comic did he work for?
3 Give the name of the church in which Chad set up the first Samaritan telephone service.
4 How did newspapers help him start his work?
5 How many Samaritan branches have been opened in Britain and Ireland?
6 How many calls and visits do The Samaritans receive each year?
7 What does The Samaritans' Flying Squad do?
8 What are the first six words a telephone caller to The Samaritans hears?
9 Why did a group of young Samaritans form a team to visit pop festivals?
10 What was Chad's advice to a man who wanted to prevent a girl committing suicide?

B Think through

These questions need longer answers. Think about them, and then try to write two or three sentences in answer to each one. You may look up the story again to help you.

1 What made Chad Varah decide to take every chance of talking to young people about their problems?
2 What was the "small miracle" with which he began his work?
3 Why did he call his organisation "The Samaritans"?
4 What does the Samaritan term "befriending" mean? How do The Samaritans put it into practice?
5 What were some of the different problems that people phoned Chad about?
6 What sort of people are the volunteers?
7 How does a Samaritan centre work?
8 What happens when a client rings The Samaritans?

25

C Talk about

Here are some questions for you to discuss together. Try to give reasons for what you say or think. Try to find out all the different opinions which people have about each question.

1 What do you think are the main difficulties that face young people today? Should parents and teachers try to give them more help?

2 How can you best help someone who has a difficult problem? Does having a religious faith benefit people in trouble?

3 Should sex education be given in schools? Would it be better in a biology or a religious education lesson?

4 Why do some people want to commit suicide? What can be done to prevent people taking such action? Should people be allowed to take their own lives?

5 What special qualities do you think are needed to make a good Samaritan volunteer? Is Chad Varah right in not offering his clients Christian comfort?

D Find out

Choose one or two of the subjects below and find out all you can about them. You will find books about them in your school or public library. Newspapers, especially local ones, will also be useful.

1 *The telephone*

(a) Find out about the life and work of Alexander Graham Bell, the inventor of the telephone. How did other scientists contribute to his invention?

(b) Make notes and drawings to show how a telephone works.

(c) Discover all you can about the invention of Morse, radio and television.

2 *Telephone services*

(a) Make a list of the telephone services offered by the Post Office.

(b) Find out about other groups that offer telephone services. writing to organisations like Release and National Children's Homes (see p. 28 for the addresses of Release and National Children's Homes).

(c) Try to find out what phone-in services are available in your area; they may be run by local churches or by the local council.

3 *Young people's problems*
(a) Make a list of the problems that face young people today.
(b) Interview people who could help to solve young people's problems, such as parents, teachers and youth club leaders. Write your findings in a book.

4 *The City of London*
(a) Find out about London in the days of the Romans and draw a map of the Roman wall and gates.
(b) Write about the Fire of London (1666).
(c) Find out about Sir Christopher Wren and the churches he built.
(d) Draw a plan of St Paul's Cathedral, name the different parts and write a description.
(e) Find out about some of the other famous buildings in the City of London, such as the Tower of London, the Mansion House, the Stock Exchange and the Guildhall.

5 *Saving life*
The Red Cross and the R.N.L.I. (Royal National Life-boat Institution) are organisations specifically founded to save life. Other groups, such as the police, nurses, fire brigades, mountain rescue teams and air rescue services, are also involved with saving life.

Choose one or two of the groups listed above and find out as much as you can about their work. Cut out newspaper items that give accounts of the kinds of work they do. (The addresses of the Red Cross and the R.N.L.I. are on p. 28, in case you would like to write to them for information about their work.)

USEFUL INFORMATION

Addresses

The General Office of
The Samaritans
17 Uxbridge Road
Slough SL1 1SN

*(Look up the address
of the local branch of
The Samaritans in your
telephone directory.)*

Royal National Life-boat
Institution
202 Lambeth Road
London SE1 7JW.

The British Red Cross
Society
9 Grosvenor Crescent
London SW1X 7EJ.

Family Network Organiser
National Children's Homes
85 Highbury Park
London N5 1UD.

Release
1 Elgin Avenue
London W9 3PR.

N.B. It is best if only one person in each class writes off for information. Remember to enclose a stamped, addressed envelope for the reply. A postal order for 50p would also be helpful, if you want plenty of material.

More books to read

Answers to Suicide, by various authors (Constable) (T).
Is Anyone There? edited by Monica Dickens and Rosemary Sutcliff (Penguin/Peacock) (T).
The Samaritans in the 80s, edited by Chad Varah (Constable) (T).
Someone to Turn to, by David Arthur (Nelson, In Focus series) (P).
World Saves Lives, by Maurice Rickards (Longman Young Books, World series) (P/T).

(T) = suitable for teachers and older pupils
(P) = suitable for younger pupils

Packs

Youth Communication Project, edited by Anthony Lawton. A folder containing detailed information about the work of The Samaritans, with a book list, posters and ideas for projects. Available from all branches of The Samaritans.

With Us in Mind, edited by Kathy West and Ann Griffith (CSV/MIND). A kit with information about mental illness and mental handicap. Ideas for projects, and a book and film list, are included. Available from CSV, 237 Pentonville Road, London N1 9NG.

Film

Can I Help You? (30 min), colour. One of several films made by The Samaritans about their work. Illustrated with several made-up case histories. Viewings can be arranged through any branch of The Samaritans.